Do You Want To Be An Actor?

The Reviews Are In

"I really needed this book!"
 Elizabeth Seldon, Actress

"What a great idea!"
 Shelly Parisi, Las Vegas Entertainer

"Smart. Useful. A terrific actors' tool."
 Lance Taubold, Actor

"It should be handed to every actor that comes to town."
 Greg Barret, Talent Manager

"I want every one of my clients to buy this book and refer to it often."
 Christine Low, Low Artists Talent

"A prerequisite to your career."
 Ellen Richards, Casting Director

Do You Want To Be An Actor?

Do You Want To Be An Actor?
101 Answers To Your Questions About Breaking Into The Biz

© Copyright 2001 / 2013 Richard Devin

All Right Reserved. Except for the inclusion of brief passages quoted in reviews, no part of this book may be reproduced or transmitted in any form or by any means, electronic or mechanical, including photocopying, recording or by any information storage and retrieval system without prior permission in writing of the publishers:

13Thirty Books
1377 Temporale Drive
Henderson, Nevada 89052

Library of Congress Cataloging-in-Publication Data

Do you want to be an actor?: 101 answers to your questions about breaking into the "biz" / [compiled by] Richard Devin
     p.cm

Includes bibliographical references

ISBN – 13: 978-0615835105
ISBN – 10: 0615835104

1. Acting - Vocational guidance. I Devin, Richard

PN2055 .D62 2002   2001059820
792'.028'023- - dc21

Do You Want To Be An Actor?

Do You Want To Be An Actor?

101 Answers To Your Questions
About Breaking Into The
Biz

Richard Devin

www.13thirtybooks.com

13Thirty Books

Do You Want To Be An Actor?

Foreword

Chapter One
Introduction   *9*

Chapter Two
Glossary   *12*

Chapter Three
Getting Started   *19*

Chapter Four
Questions – Answers   *29*

Chapter Five
What To Do Next   *135*

List of Contributors   *137*

Do You Want To Be An Actor?

Do You Want To Be An Actor?

I wish to thank:

Jeff Depew for his editorial assistance.
Scott Williams for the original cover art for the first edition.
Lance Taubold for his continued support.
The many show business professionals who contributed their time and efforts to this book.

And

I dedicate this book to the memory of two wonderful friends and great film, TV and Broadway actors:

Paul Cira and Paul "Wes" Skelly

Do You Want To Be An Actor?

When I began to put this book together, I was working as a personal manager to actors and still pursuing my own personal dreams of becoming a working actor. Now, some years later I find myself sitting on the other side of the desk – as a theatrical agent in a well-known and respected agency in Los Angeles. It has been an eye opening experience. I see now what actors are up against from a very different perspective "If only I'd had this insight when I was beginning my journey!" The agents view on actors and acting. That, my friends, will be the subject for another book.

And so for now, I turn you to the pages that follow, hopefully you will glean a fount of information from these pages that will set you off on the journey of *your* dreams and hasten the reality of you becoming a working actor.

                        Break – a – Leg
                        Richard Devin

Do You Want To Be An Actor?

"Life is like a box of chocolates; you never know what you're gonna' get."

Forrest Gump

Do You Want To Be An Actor?

Introduction

Thousands of hopefuls enter into the "Biz" every year, some will make it big, and some will make a living at it, and most will drop out before five years are up. It is a selfish business. Its demands are many. The rewards can be few, but when you are rewarded by being cast in a film, television show or stage production . . . nothing can ever beat that feeling.

When I decided to become an actor, my mind reeled with hundreds of questions. I assume that you have many of the same questions or you would not have picked up this book. The questions that you have now and that all aspiring and new actors will have for some time to come have not changed since I first entered into this business, but the answers have. That is why I went directly to the source – Actors, Photographers, Acting Coaches, Directors, Producers, Casting Directors and Agents – and asked them the same questions that you and actors from all over the country have been asking me.

While giving seminars, based on my book, *Actors' Resumes: The Definitive Guidebook* – which has become the industry "bible" to proper formatting and marketing of an actor through his resume – I have had the great opportunity to meet many wonderful aspiring and up and coming actors. The actors' questions generally start with comments about resumes and marketing but soon move to; "What do I do when _____?" You fill in the blank.

The questions asked at those seminars were the genesis for this book. An actor would ask a specific question that I and the others on the panel would have differing opinions to. So when I got back to LA, I'd call a casting director friend or an agent friend or a producer friend (you get the picture) and ask them the same questions that the actor had asked me. Then I'd either call or write or e-mail the actor with the answer that the talent buyer had given.

Do You Want To Be An Actor?

Soon, I started receiving questions "on-line" from actors that I had met and from others who saw my responses on the web. I went through the same processes with them. From this I compiled a list of the most frequently asked questions by new and aspiring actors. I then asked talent buyers (casting directors, agents, producers, managers, directors), Actors, Acting Coaches and Photographers to answer the questions on this list.

The following pages contain the answers to these questions and yours. I asked Talent, Talent Buyers, Acting Coaches and Photographer from all over the country, so that the responses would reflect every geographic area. I sent out questionnaires randomly to industry professionals. I wanted to get answers to your questions from those who were truly interested in responding. From those who had a desire to help. And from those who remember what it is like to be where you are now. In most cases the name of the talent or talent buyer who answered the question is listed on top of the page. Some "big name" individuals asked to remain anonymous and I have, of course honored their wishes.

The questions and answers contained on these pages are sometimes tough but always honest. If you're thinking about breaking into this business you need to read on.

When I first thought about becoming an actor, I did not have this book . . . you do!

I hope these questions and answers point you in the right direction and that soon, you'll be "walking the boards" of the next big Broadway play or musical, or maneuvering the somewhat chaotic sets of a television studio, sound stage or location.

The very best of luck to all,
Richard Devin

Do You Want To Be An Actor?

"...a way of life based on one simple rule: Be kind."

Lost Horizon

Do You Want To Be An Actor?

Glossary

3/4 Shot
A photograph showing the body of the actor from the knees up.

8 by 10
A photograph having the approximate measurements of 8 inches wide by 10 inches long. An actor's "calling card" usually black and white. Also known as a "headshot."

Acting Coach
An acting teacher.

Adjustment
To make a change in the reading or audition as directed to by a producer, agent, casting director or director.

AEA
Actors Equity Association. The union of stage managers and stage actors.

AFTRA
The American Federation of Television and Radio Artists. The union that represents television actors, broadcast journalists and on-air radio personnel.

Agent
The person who represents: sells, promotes and negotiates on your behalf to the talent buyers.

Atmosphere
Background or extra performer.

Audit
A free session or class that an actor may sit in on in order to observe the way an acting coach or teacher directs his class.

Do You Want To Be An Actor?

Audition
To "try out" for a part or role.

Background
An extra. Non-speaking role.

Blind Submission
When talent submits his or her picture and resume to a talent buyer without specifying what the picture is for or to a specific person.

Body Shot
A photograph showing the complete or nearly complete body of the actor.

Booking Out
The term used when an actor tells his or her representation, manager or agent, that the actor will not be available to work or audition during a certain time frame, i.e.; "I'm going back home for the holidays so I booked out with my agent for two weeks."

Casting Director
The person who acts as a liaison between the talent, the representation and the producer. The person who aids the producer and/or director in the casting of a production.

Casting Society of America
The organization of professional casting directors.

CD
Abbreviation for casting director.

Cold Reading
An audition or reading given by the actor when the actor has not had much time to be directed or work with the material.

Do You Want To Be An Actor?

Commission
A fee, usually a percentage, that an agent or manager earns from monies that the talent is paid for work performed.

Congress of Personal Managers
The organization of personal managers.

COPM
Abbreviation for Congress of Personal Managers.

Credits
A list of work that the talent had been hired (with or without payment) to perform.

CSA
Abbreviation for the Casting Society of America.

Director
The person, who leads, manipulates or otherwise controls the movement of the actors and/or the camera.

Extra
Talent who perform, without dialogue in motion pictures and television. They populate the set or scene, adding atmosphere.

Franchised
An agency that has been "licensed" by one or more of the actors' unions.

Freelance
Talent that is not signed to one specific manager or agent, but instead is represented by one or more agent or manager on a non-contractual basis.

General
Common abbreviation for "general interview."

Do You Want To Be An Actor?

General Interview
When talent is called in to meet the talent buyer on a one on one basis. Not necessarily an audition. More like – a get to know you – session.

Glossy
A common term used to indicate an actor's headshot.

Going to Producers
A call back. After the initial audition, the talent, that the casting director has decided is right for the role, is taken to the producers. This is where an actor gets the job.

Handle
To represent.

Headshot
An actor's 8 by 10, glossy or calling card. A photograph of the actor that is given to talent buyers.

Hip Pocket
To be represented without the benefit of a contract. Quite often an agent will accept a number of pictures and resumes from the talent to submit to casting directors to "see what happens" before signing the actor.

Interview
A meeting with a talent buyer in which the talent does not necessarily audition but instead has a conversation with the talent buyer.

List
The names or the clients that an agent has on its client roster.

Lithograph
A type of photographic reproduction. Uses a system that is grainier than photographic reproduction but is considerably less expensive than using photographic paper.

Do You Want To Be An Actor?

Manager
A personal manager, someone who represents talent to the talent buyers. Acts in a close relationship with the talent and as a liaison between the talent and the talent buyers.

Producer
The person or persons who is/are in charge of the entire production. He hires, fires, schedules and budgets for the production. There is quite often a team of producers i.e.; Executive Producer, Co-Producer, Assistant Producer, Associate Producer, Coordinating Producer, Line Producer, Directing Producer.

Representation Commercial
The agent or agency that negotiates and promotes talent for work in television and radio commercials as well as for print advertisements.

Representation Theatrical
An agent or agency that negotiates and promotes talent for film and television and/or stage.

SAG
Abbreviation for the Screen Actors Guild.

SAG Card
The card that members of the Screen Actors Guild have to prove membership in that union, i.e.; "Do you have your card?"

Scene Study
Classes that emphasize the scenes within a script where an actor finds and reacts to the moments and transitions.

Screen Actors Guild
The union that represents actors for television, film and video.

Do You Want To Be An Actor?

Session
The time and place where casting directors and producers meet with talent to audition.

Showcase
A performance by one or more actors, in which talent buyers are invited to see the actors perform scenes or monologues. Quite often these, performances have become lavish productions where valet parking, along with food and drink are the norm. Actors generally pay for these productions.

Sides
The portion of the script that talent is given for an audition.

Sign
The common term for talent that an agent or manger has agreed to represent, i.e.; "Are you signed with that agency?"

Survival Job
Any employment that is outside of acting. The way talent makes money to pay the rent, eat, and put gas in the car, etc., until the big break comes.

Talent
You, the actor!

Working Actor
An actor who makes his living from acting. What you soon will be!

Do You Want To Be An Actor?

"I'll make him an offer he can't refuse."

The Godfather

Do You Want To Be An Actor?

Getting Started

"If an actor does not know *himself*... how can his market?"

I can't remember the name of the producer I met at a party a couple of years ago at an "A" list actor's house in Pacific Palisades. He was talking to an actor – who was trying to sell himself as a Brad Pitt type when he was really a Chris Farley type. The producer was explaining to this young thespian that he should go out and *find himself*, not the metaphysical meaning of finding oneself, but the "where is my market" meaning.

The producer happened to be casting a film at the time so – of course – every actor in the room was vying for his attention. The actor, who currently had the producer cornered, was suggesting that he was just right for a particular role in the upcoming film. Much to the actor's jubilance the producer thought so too. Only the producer suggested the "character" role not the romantic lead. The actor could not understand why the producer did not see him as the leading man. After some debate the producer suggested to the actor that he ask everyone at the party what type of roles they think he should play.

In the end the actor got his answer and I got an idea.

That idea turned into the worksheets that follow. Using them has helped me a tremendous amount. As a matter of fact, I know of several coaches and image consultants who now use a worksheet very similar to these for their clients.

The following worksheets will help you, *find yourself*. It's a very easy and eye opening processes that can save you years of struggle as an actor.

To make the most of the worksheets, follow this simple process. First make about twenty copies of each worksheet page. Then hand the pages out to some people you know and *more importantly* too many people that you do not know. Go to the mall, the corner, anywhere that's safe and where you'll get a good cross section of people. You might want to

Do You Want To Be An Actor?

bring along a friend to ask people to fill out the worksheets while you stand or sit nearby. Have your friend tell people that you are an up and coming actor and that your marketing people are doing some research into which future films and television shows you should be cast in.

Now, have those people mark on the sheets what traits they "see" as you and in what movies or television shows they could "see" you being in. None of these people should actually speak with you prior to filling out the worksheets. It is best for you if people mark what they "sense" as being you and in what films and television shows you should be in based on their observation of you alone.

After the worksheets have been filled in, it's perfectly all right to speak to them; it would even be nice of you to thank each of the respondents. I can't tell you how many actors have had people ask for their autographs, so bring along some pictures to hand out.

Remember to save one page of each work sheet for yourself and mark the way you "see" yourself.

When the worksheets have been filled out, compare the way you "see yourself" and the way others did. You might be very surprised!

Do You Want To Be An Actor?

Who Am I? / What Am I?

DINGBAT
TOUGH
INFANTILE
RURAL
SHY
VIXEN
CLASSY
THREATENING
OBNOXIOUS
SULTRY
CUTE
NATURAL
DOWN
HANDSOME
STOCKY
MYSTICAL
COMMANDING
BOHEMIAN
IMPOSING
UNHEALTHY
TECHNICAL
INTENSE
TIMID
BESPECTACLED
EXPLOSIVE
LOST
SNOOTY
WASP
BENEVOLENT
INDIFFERENT
VIOLENT
LANKY
DEFINED

Do You Want To Be An Actor?

CRUDE
SAVVY
SYMPATHETIC
VOLUPTUOUS
IMPOSING
SASSY
WEATHERED
GLAMOROUS
SENSUOUS
PRECOCIOUS
DESPERATE
MENACING
REFLECTIVE
GENTLE
UNSCRUPULOUS
TALKATIVE
TENACIOUS
INSULTING
BLACK
PURPLE
TOMBOY
BUSTY
INNOCENT
URBAN
RESERVED
FAKE
PREDICTABLE
OFFENSIVE
EXOTIC
UNIQUE
NO-NONSENSE
OBSESSED
INSANE
FLAMBOYANT

Do You Want To Be An Actor?

ARISTOCRATIC
WISDOM
OPEN
FRAIL
FORMIDABLE
PALE
SEEDY
PASSIONATE
CURT
BLUE COLLAR
SPONTANEOUS
AVERAGE
SCIENTIFIC
GEEKY
POWERFUL
GRACIOUS
AGGRESSIVE
ECCENTRIC
ATTRACTIVE
TROUBLED
DARK
IMPULSIVE
WHIMSICAL
TRANQUIL
SOPHISTICATED
MISCHIEVOUS
SPIRITED
FAST
GRUFF
PRAGMATIC
EXPRESSIVE
PERKY
SWEET
BITCHY

Do You Want To Be An Actor?

IMPATIENT
CONGENIAL
DUMB
WHITE
PINK
LONER
ARROGANT
ABRASIVE
STUD
WILD
CYNICAL
RELAXED
CAUTIOUS
TRENDY
WHINER
WINNER
LOSER
WIRY
INTELLIGENT
ENERGETIC
ELEGANT
SARCASTIC
CALM
TYRANNICAL
GROUCHY
LIKABLE
BOYISH
GIRLISH
WELL BRED
EXAGGERATED
FIERCE
HOT
INATTENTIVE
DIGNIFIED

Do You Want To Be An Actor?

INTROSPECTIVE
WHITE COLLAR
HIP
GUILTY
CONFIDENT
INTIMIDATING
VIVID
FLEDGLING
CLEAN-CUT
INSECURE
SEXUAL
UNSTABLE
COUNTRY
HICK
QUICK
EAGER
ANGRY
JADED
SELF INVOLVED
QUICK WITTED
STREET SMART
SLY
BLUE
YELLOW
BROWN
ENGAGING
CHARISMATIC
MEEK
INSENSITIVE
INCORRIGIBLE
TRASHY
SEXY
FEMININE
NERVOUS

Do You Want To Be An Actor?

RICH
OFF-BEAT
KINKY
ORNERY
ATHLETIC
ALL AMERICAN
GOOD
DEDICATED
BURLY
FUNNY
VICTIM
SLENDER
SKINNY
SEVERE
RAKISH
MOUSY
ATTENTIVE
SILLY
DISTANT
ANALYTICAL
SUAVE
CONFUSED
CLEVER
PLAIN
ABUSIVE
TIRED
RESERVED
RUGGED
CANKEROUS
SELFISH
SUBDUED
VULNERABLE
BAWDY
DOGMATIC

Do You Want To Be An Actor?

CHARMING
POUTY
GULLIBLE
PARASITIC
AMBITIOUS
FIREY
GREGARIOUS
VIVACIOUS
RED
GREEN
ORANGE
DIM WITTED

Do You Want To Be An Actor?

"You want answers?"
- "I want the truth!"
- "You can't handle the truth!"

                        A Few Good Men

Do You Want To Be An Actor?

Questions – Answers

Agent
Johnny Johnston

What do actors do to turn you off at an interview?

It is incredibly unprofessional and a real turn off when an actor comes into to my office asking me to represent them and then they don't even bring a picture and resume with them.

Author's Note:

If an actor has sent in a picture and resume to an agent, a casting director, a director, a producer – anyone – asking for an audition or an interview, that actor should always bring along another headshot. It's the professional thing to do! And as you can see – simple things can be a "real turn off."

Do You Want To Be An Actor?

Agent
Johnny Johnston
Quality Artists

What do actors do to turn you off at an interview?

I really dislike an actor who bad mouths his or her current agent when they're interviewing with me for representation. Remember, just because your current agent and I are in different offices, and because we vie for the same talent, the same auditions and the same jobs for our clients, doesn't mean that me and the agent you are bad mouthing aren't friends!

Author's Note:

It's a small town when it comes to this business and everyone generally knows everyone else. When the office closes and the lights are turned out, we all go to the same places and you can bet that your current agent may hear from someone else just what it is that you said about him or her in another agent's office. In the second world war there was a saying that "loose lips, sink ships," now they can ruin careers. Be nice. Always!

Do You Want To Be An Actor?

Agent
Johnny Johnston
Quality Artists

What do actors do to turn you off at an interview?

I ask actors that I'm interviewing to tell me something about themselves that has nothing to do with acting or the business. I'm always amazed that most actors cannot think of a thing to say that doesn't have to do with acting. It makes me ask myself, "If they have nothing going on in their lives aside from acting, what can they bring to the part?"

Author's Note:

Always be prepared to talk about yourself. Agents want to know about your acting experience and they'll ask. But there is more to life than acting. Talk about your hobbies, something that you saw in the paper that day or something that you just bought at the store. Tell them who you are by the way you see life. It will help your agent find what he or she likes about you and it will help sell you.

Do You Want To Be An Actor?

Agent
Bert Charles
The Charles Agency

Can you suggest a way for an actor to market himself to the talent buyers to enhance his chances of being called in for an audition or for an interview?

I always tell talent that there is a thin line between persistence and annoyance, which must be cautiously walked. It is always good to do something different or something that will get you noticed, but keep the previous statement in mind.

The last thing an actor wants to do is affect his or her chances negatively by shocking the talent buyer or by annoying them. For example, I recently received a picture and resume in the mail – on the back of the envelope the person had hand written a note. It read, "Be sure to trash this picture face up." When I saw this I immediately laughed and before I even opened the envelope I knew that I would, at the very least, interview this person.

If you are going to market yourself to talent buyers try not to be so serious all the time. Think along the lines of the lighter side. The agent or casting director may not call you in at first, but if they see your picture enough and they continuously get cute or fun little notes or letters from you, they may be more inclined to take a chance and call you in.

Do You Want To Be An Actor?

Agent
Bert Charles
The Charles Agency

Can you suggest a way for an actor to enhance his chances of being called in for the audition or the interview?

Don't ever appear to be desperate.

Author's Note:

No one wants to be with people who are desperate. Like the old saying, "Everyone loves a winner." Be that winner. Keep a winning attitude always. If you're on the set longer than you were supposed to be or the audition is running late – keep your chin up. The powers that be will remember you and you'll work more because of it.

Don't go in saying "I've got to have this job." It will work against you – sure we would all like to get the job or the audition or that special agent or manager, but being desperate is not the way to get it.

Do You Want To Be An Actor?

Agent
Bert Charles
The Charles Agency

Can you suggest a way for an actor to market himself to the talent buyers to enhance his chances of being called in for the audition or the interview?

Don't submit yourself for a role if you are not the type that the casting director is looking for. Don't waste the casting director's time on submissions if you are not right.

Author's Note:

In film and television, a nineteen year old girl is not going to play a grandmother, even if you did do it in the last production of your high school play and you were a big hit. You must be right on for the role or fit the description of the character as closely as possible. There will be many actors submitted who will be right on for the role and the casting director won't call you in if you're not right. Save your picture, the postage and the talent buyer's time. In doing so talent buyers will grow to respect you and when they see your headshot in the stack of pictures and resumes that have come in, yours will get pulled.

Do You Want To Be An Actor?

Agent
Bert Charles
The Charles Agency

Can you suggest a way for an actor to market himself to the talent buyers to enhance his chances of being called in for the audition or the interview?

Be patient! This is a numbers game. The longer you're around and the more times that the talent buyers see you, the better your chances of working.

Do You Want To Be An Actor?

Agent
Bert Charles
The Charles Agency

Can you suggest a way for an actor to market himself to the talent buyers to enhance his chances of being called in for the audition or the interview?

Remember the "BUSINESS" of "SHOW BUSINESS."

Always be courteous and professional with whomever you may meet or talk to, whether on the telephone, at an audition or at a party. It's not unusual for an agent or a casting director to answer the telephone or greet you when you walk into their office. If you seem rude or unprofessional, say "bye-bye" to any chance for an interview. You never know who you might be talking to or meet.

As an agent, I only want to work with people who are polite, fun and professional. Not only are they representing themselves at every audition and to every casting director, producer or director they meet, they're also representing me and my agency. If an actor embarrasses himself, he's hurting my reputation and that of the other clients I handle. If he is professional and is able to work with others, he is helping his chances of working and my chances to get him the auditions.

Do You Want To Be An Actor?

Agent
Bert Charles
The Charles Agency

Can you suggest a way for an actor to market himself to the talent buyers to enhance his chances of being called in for the audition or the interview?

Work for yourself. Many actors will "sit back" after getting an agent or manager, waiting for the next call. Motivate yourself. Send letters when you have just signed with a new agent or manager or that you have just booked a job. This is a perfect way to remind the talent buyers that you are "Alive and well."

Author's Note:

"Promotion, promotion and promotion," is what my good friend, Lady Barrow, Kathryn Falk, CEO and Founder of Romantic Times Magazine, says to authors about their books. The same holds true for actors.

Do You Want To Be An Actor?

Agent
Bert Charles
The Charles Agency

Can you suggest a way for an actor to market himself to the talent buyers to enhance his chances of being called in for the audition or the interview?

Make your headshot GREAT! It is one of the most important tools that you have. It should be high quality, recent and above all it should LOOK LIKE YOU! If a talent buyer calls you in and you don't look like your headshot, they will not be happy.

Author's Note:

Find a good photographer and get the best shots you can. You don't need to spend thousands of dollars to get a good shot. A lot of money spent on pictures is not a guarantee that the pictures will do the trick. On the other hand if the photographer you like is one that costs a bit more than the guy down the street, it may be for a good reason.

Take your time in choosing a photographer. Look at pictures of other actors and ask them who took their pictures. Ask your agent or manager which photographers they like. Ask the casting director you're auditioning for if they have a moment to suggest a good photographer. If they know the name of one or two, it's because they like his or her work and they took the time to find out who the photographer was. Check out the books of many different photographers and ask them questions. If you get along well with them your chances of getting a great shot are immensely enhanced.

When reproducing your picture, bear in mind what your agent or manager likes or dislikes about photographic reproductions. Some think lithographs are fine, other don't like them at all. Some want glossy shots, others like pearl or matte finishes. Ask them. They'll appreciate that you took the time to consider what they need to market you.

Do You Want To Be An Actor?

Agent
Bert Charles
The Charles Agency
11950 Ventura Blvd., 3
Studio City, CA   91604

Can you suggest a way for an actor to market himself to the talent buyers to enhance his chances of being called in for the audition or the interview?

Never "sit" on your acting ability. Practice and hone your craft. There is always someone out there who is driven and they will inevitably win out over you if you do not keep up on your craft. Just like the hinge that is not used, you too will become rusty. Keep active. Strive for perfection.

Do You Want To Be An Actor?

Actor
Grace Renn

Should an actor go to his audition with the sides memorized?

If possible, yes. The casting director looks for professional actors who not only know the material but also make acting their priority. The worst thing that can happen at an audition is to be in a very dramatic moment in the script or a wonderful punch line in a comedy scene and have to struggle with the lines. By being familiar with the material to the point of having it memorized you can make choices for your character. Anyone can recite the lines. It's the choices and commitment you make as an actor that effect the reading of the lines that are going to get you noticed. And yes, always hold the sides while you're auditioning, in case you need to refer to them.

Author's Note:

Beware of going to an audition with your lines so memorized that you cannot make adjustments to your reading because you are so set in the lines. You are at an audition to audition, so there is danger in having your lines completely memorized. It may be best to reach the point when you have become very familiarized with the lines. This gives you the ability to adjust the reading and mold the character more to what the talent buyer has in mind. We never want the talent buyer to think that what you're doing is giving him or her, a performance. You are auditioning, after all and the talent buyer wants to know that this reading can go somewhere. If you come in with the lines completely memorized and don't use the sides – what else can you be doing but performing. And what if the casting director doesn't like your performance... you're out of the picture, literally. I often tell actors, "Go in with your sides memorized and then act as though you don't."

Do You Want To Be An Actor?

Actor
Grace Renn

If an actor would like to have a manager handle his career, when should he or she look for a manager?

Finding the right manager to push your career along is one of the greater challenges for the beginning actor. If you think of yourself (the actor) as a product, you want to be able to trust the salesperson with that product, and who not only understands your product, but knows how best to sell you to the talent buyers.

Getting a good manager is a not easy. It's a "Catch 22." The manager you're interviewing with will want to know if you have an agent. If you don't, they will have to find one for you. Most managers already have working actors as clients and they don't have time to cultivate someone new with no credits, little experience and no agent.

To get a manager you have to show them how marketable you are. And never give up. I had to interview with eight managers before I found one that would represent me. I had to find who was right for me and who I was right for. It took over a year for me to find the right manager and I had my SAG card, credits and a good agent. Remember it's the challenge of the process.

Do You Want To Be An Actor?

Actor
Tom Urich

Do you believe that an actor needs a manager?

At the beginning of one's career, if the actor has a good agent, he does not need a manager. In my 36 years in the business, I've had only 4 agents. My first agent was an agent – manager – confidante – friend and sister. If you're lucky enough to find an agent that cares about you the way my first agent cared about me, then you don't need a manager. When you become really successful a manager can help in the decisions you make for the direction of you career. Plus, many managers will push and shove to get you seen when many agents can't or don't have the time and inclination to.

Do You Want To Be An Actor?

Actor
Tom Urich

Must an actor take a class that the agent has referred him to in order to sign with that agent?

Absolutely not! If the agency is any good at all and reputable they will accept you no matter where you may choose to take class.

Author's Note:

A good agent looks for clients who are interested in perfecting their craft and making themselves as marketable as possible. They should be happy to see that you are studying with any reputable acting coach. But you may wish to bear in mind that the agent may suggest acting coaches to you without requiring you to study with them before they will sign you.

Do You Want To Be An Actor?

Manager
Frank Campana
Personal Management

Should an actor do extra work?

Yes. An actor should gain experience any way that he or she can. Do atmosphere/background work in films and television as a way of learning what happens on a set.

Author's Note:

Pay attention when you're on the set. Take a moment to ask a grip or gaffer what it is that they do. Listen and learn. Hopefully, you won't have to remain a background actor very long and all the information you gleaned from the techs and other actors on the set will come in very handy to your acting career.

Do You Want To Be An Actor?

Manager
Frank Campana
Personal Management

What are a few ways, other than acting classes, that an actor can learn?

Go to the theater as often as you can and see as many films and television shows as possible. Watch the actors. Note how they move and what they say. Should you be lucky enough to get a speaking role, pay attention to the director. You can learn more from a good director and a good production than from years of acting classes.

Do You Want To Be An Actor?

Manager
Frank Campana
Personal Management

The actors' unions set an agent's commission at 10 percent. What commission does a manager receive?

Managers' fees or commissions are usually 15% to 20%, but they can be negotiated higher or lower by the client (talent) and the manager. For example, Col. Parker, Elvis Presley's manager received a commission on all of Elvis' income of 50%.

Do You Want To Be An Actor?

Actress
Mary-Rachel Foot

How should an actor prepare for a move to New York or Los Angeles in search of an acting career?

When I moved from NYC to LA about 3 1/2 years ago, I didn't know what to expect. I knew I wanted a career in the Entertainment Industry and I always loved acting, but I wasn't sure how to approach it.

Instead of leaping into the acting world right away, I got a job as an administrator at a sound design post production facility. While working there I was able to learn about all areas of the business and also meet all kinds of professionals from producers to directors, editors to musicians, agents to actors. I observed everything. I wanted to get a feel for the industry before I jumped in the pool. About a year and half went by and I started to get antsy – I wanted to do more to create, to get out of a 9 -5 job. So, I did. I got into an acting class and from there slowly started looking for a manager and an agent and I started auditioning.

Something to keep in mind if you are looking to move is that acting is a process you can't just decide one day to do, and think that you could book a movie in a week! That's completely unrealistic. If that does happen to someone (and in this business it could) that person is very lucky. It's not the norm. Acting is a highly competitive career (business) choice. Prepare yourself mentally. Know why you have chosen this as your career; is it just for fame? Forget it. You have to love the art because rejection is a big part of the process. Know who you are and be grounded. Treat people with respect but don't be a people pleaser. Watch out for 'skeezebags' that are only interested in one thing ... and it never works. Be prepared to give financially to your career. It's expensive to promote yourself from headshots, mailings, photographer fees, acting classes, makeup and so much more. You're going to work hard and have a busy schedule. Have integrity, tenacity and good morals. Study, study, study. Although acting classes are expensive, it's worth it to work on your instrument. When you're not "working," work on getting great

Do You Want To Be An Actor?

headshots. You're only as good as your headshot.

Los Angeles is a very lonely city. Have some sort of support system to fall back on. I started my own acting group and for a year ten actors had a place to discuss their successes, fears, hopes and failures. Exercise, stay in shape both mentally and physically. Don't get caught working the "Hollywood" party scene. It's more destructive then helpful.

At some point you will undoubtedly feel stressed and wonder why you are here. That is part of the process. We all do it. Do other things that you enjoy. It helps keeps you fresh. As an actor be prepared to discover things about yourself that you never knew existed. You may have to go to these places to fulfill a character. The audience will want to see that. Go for it all.

Good Luck!

Do You Want To Be An Actor?

Actress
Mary-Rachel Foot

Should an actor go to an audition with the sides memorized?

Sometimes your agent or manager will call you at the last minute for an audition. This makes it very difficult to learn your sides, especially when you pick up the sides when you get to the audition. That's why cold reading is an important part of the auditioning process. However, when you do have time to read the script and work on it, it is definitely a good idea to do so. The more familiar you are with the material the more room it gives you to work on the character. The casting director will usually be able to tell in the first thirty seconds if you're right for the part. Definitely memorize your lines but always go into the audition with the sides in your hands, just in case you forget a line. It's okay to refer to your sides. Also, if you're that good when you're just auditioning think about how good you will be in the role. This is what casting directors like to see in an actor.

Do You Want To Be An Actor?

Casting Director
Judith Jacobs

What do you think of plastic surgery to enhance an actor's appearance or to correct a problem?

There is a major difference between improving a truly problem area for the camera, maintaining your look (remember you are a product) and going overboard.

We all know stars or sports celebrities that have had so much work done on them that we can hardly recognize them anymore.

No one even remembers Dean Martin's old nose ... or check out old video tape on David Schwimmer for Northwestern, you'll understand the comparison. Demi Moore has had three children (so far) and has been oft voted best famous body – nature can do just so much. Bob Barker can't stop smiling, but he has looked fabulous on camera for over 40 years. The reality is that the camera not only records your changing physicality, but often exaggerates every flaw. Recognizing what can be a fine line between character and caricature can mean the difference between "oooooos," "ahhhhhhhs" and whispers.

Do You Want To Be An Actor?

Casting Director
Judith Jacobs

What do you think of plastic surgery to enhance an actor's appearance or to correct a problem?

I remember several years ago putting one of my favorite regulars on tape during an audition. She had always had bags under her eyes, but now that she was moving well past forty, the bags under her eyes made her look worn and tired. After her audition, I brought this up to her. She said that her agent had already mentioned it and that my bringing it up was definitely putting her in the direction of having some work done on her eyes.

She called one day to tell me that she was about to have the surgery. Now, she is still working and appears regularly in films, on television and in commercials. If you think that plastic surgery will change your life and solve all of life's problems, you're wrong, and you will be greatly disappointed as well as 'mucho dinero' poorer! But if you have heard from several important sources that your nose, for instance, is photographing poorly, or if there is a major imbalance in your features then it may be a worthwhile investment. And this is one area where it would not be a bright idea to be a bargain hunter! Interview several surgeons, perhaps someone who has worked on people that you know. After all it's not just your face, body or career . . . it's your life!

Do You Want To Be An Actor?

Casting Director
Judith Jacobs

Tell us about a major "no-no" that actors do at an audition.

This can include everything from coming in unprepared (without a current picture and resume, or dressing inappropriately) to showing up drunk, to insulting the casting director in front of everyone in the waiting room - - yep! That's just the tip of the iceberg of the experiences from over 20 years in this business.

Here's the biggie . . . basically, I find a very low percentage of great cold readers in this business, which is especially amazing considering that EVERYTHING other than theater is booked by cold readings.

My definition of cold reading is that there should be no difference between how you sound telling a friend about something that happened, and how you sound reading any script or copy. That level of risk, bringing your own vocal and physical personality to your read, never "hearing" the actor reading for them ... that's a great audition. And let's face it – you can't book the job without a terrific audition.

Do You Want To Be An Actor?

Casting Director
Judith Jacobs

What do the actors who are working or who have made it big have in common?

The one thing that the actors I have booked most over the years, as well as the ones I have worked with who have hit it big, Jill Eikenberry and Michael Tucker (LA Law), Garrett Brown (Sisters), John Goodman (Roseanne), have in common is the instinct and ability or the trained technique to bring their personality to everything they do. To quote a not (yet) famous, but very respected Chicago – New York actor, Peter Van Wagner, "Everybody's got to bring something to the party."

Do You Want To Be An Actor?

Actress
Kristine Benedict

When should an actor start his or her search for agent representation?

After studying for a few years.

I believe that the search for an agent is an ongoing process. Representation is a shared responsibility; the actor must always represent himself, the agent must share in that representation. Also, do as many plays as you can. But bear in mind that getting an agent to come and see you will depend largely on who else is in the cast and where the play is being produced.

Industry referrals seem to be the best way to gain access to an agent. If you know someone in the industry, especially a casting director, producer, director, other agent or celebrity have them write you a letter or give the agent a call and ask them to see you.

Author's Note:

You may find one that one actor wants to have agent representation at a very early stage in his career so that he and the agent work together developing a career for the actor that will result in a long and profitable relationship for both. Other actors prefer to wait until they have had substantial training and experience before pursuing representation. The choice to seek representation is an individual decision, but remember without a resume full of credits or a picture and personality that promises much, the agents that you pursue may not be looking to add to their list.

Do You Want To Be An Actor?

Agent
Audra J. Brown
Dramatic Artist Agency

What can an actor expect during the interview with you?

Expect the interview to last about an hour or less. Generally, you should be ready for a little on camera work, a cold reading to scope out your audition skills, as well as a monologue or short scene with a scene partner. Also if you have tape we may play the demo and make a few comments. Be prepared to explain further your background and experiences.

Do You Want To Be An Actor?

Manager
Greg Barrett
Greg Barrett and Associates

What can an actor expect during the interview with you?

Just be yourself! That's who we're interested in.

Do You Want To Be An Actor?

Agent
Audra J. Brown
Dramatic Artist Agency

Must an actor take a class that the agent has referred him to in order to sign with the agency?

No actor should ever feel as though he must take classes in order to sign – particularly if it is the agency that is offering the classes (for a fee of course). However, your agent will only want the best for you, his client, if he recommends classes that will assist you in your acting abilities which will in turn get you closer to landing an acting job, then it may not be a bad idea to take classes.

Understand though, that there are things you must do in order to sign with an agency, such as: keeping the agency supplied with current headshots and resumes, and keeping the agent aware of when you are in or out of town (booking out). You may also be asked to sign an agency contract.

Author's Note:

If the classes are free to the actor, why not take them? Some agencies actually do offer their clients free classes. After all, it's in the agency's best interest if the client is good.

Do You Want To Be An Actor?

Artistic Director
Carl Butto
Creative Casting & Acting

What suggestions might you have for someone moving to New York or LA in search of an acting career?

You must not say to yourself, *I'll give it a shot,* or *Maybe I'll make it,* or any other negative comment. Make sure before you leave for New York, LA or any other locale that has the industry there, you check out reputable schools and workshops. You must keep the acting muscles sharp. You should be financially set to carry yourself until you secure some employment. When you do find a "survival job," don't make it the type that expects you to make a lifelong career out of it. Instead, find a job that enables you to make the money that you need and still leave time for auditions and interviews. Be positive, sharp and confident. You must be committed to the art and allow the business to follow.

Do You Want To Be An Actor?

Artistic Director
Carl Butto
Creative Casting & Acting

What suggestions do you have for actors who become so nervous at auditions that they don't do their best?

It is necessary to begin to relax the minute you leave for your audition. Don't wait until you reach the audition. When you are working the sides don't try to memorize, but instead concentrate on creating a place for yourself. Create the space that your character is in and what you are doing. In other words, keep yourself busy with the creative process so you forget about being nervous.

Do You Want To Be An Actor?

Agent
Greg Boaldin
The Gregory Agency

What might you suggest to an actor who doesn't have many credits, but would like to find representation?

I frequently accept talent that doesn't have many credits if that person has some additional spark. It could be an interesting sellable look, a winning personality that makes people comfortable to be around or a strong drive to succeed. We try to nurture talent and work to build their credits. I think that small and medium sized markets offer wonderful opportunities for people to get the training, confidence and experience necessary to move on to bigger markets, jobs and money.

Do You Want To Be An Actor?

Agent
Greg Boaldin
The Gregory Agency

What good tip can you suggest to a newer actor?

Actors need to constantly work on growth. They need to commit themselves to getting more training and more experience, whether in the theater, television or films, and get the best tools that they can (resumes and headshots). So many times I see actors getting complacent when they are doing well in a market. They don't think about what they could be doing in their smaller markets to make themselves more appealing to a larger market. There is work to be had in every city and actors should try to tap into those opportunities where credits can be earned with less competition.

Do You Want To Be An Actor?

Agent
Greg Boaldin
The Gregory Agency

Do actors need to pay their agents in advance for representation?

I feel very strongly that actors should never pay agent money in advance. Even though this practice in more common in smaller markets, talent should either search out the agent who works strictly on commission or if need be work freelance. Think about it – if someone agrees to represent you, knowing they only get paid if you get work, that agent is going to work harder for you. If someone, who has agreed to represent you, has already been paid, what is their incentive to get you the bookings you deserve?

Actors always have to be cautious whenever they are dealing with someone involved in their career. When looking for representation, an actor should call the local TV stations or video production companies and ask them who they use or who they might recommend. Just because someone is a good model agent doesn't mean that they are a good commercial or theatrical agent. And because someone has a fancy office doesn't mean they are the best agent for you.

Actors need to be smart about their career and only work with people they trust. Part of that trust comes from knowing your agent is interested in you and not your money. This doesn't mean that there won't be expenses. Actors need to be prepared to invest in their career with the best head shots and training they can get. However, their expenses should not include an up-front fee for the agent – he should earn his commission.

Author's Note:

The agents who are franchised by the actor's unions, SAG, AFTRA, and AEA strongly prohibit an agent from charging any upfront fees for representation. Agents who are not franchised may be able to do

Do You Want To Be An Actor?

so. Check your state and local laws.

Managers on the other hand are not franchised by the unions and they may ask for upfront fees. I don't see a problem with this if the fee they are asking for will be deducted from any later commissions they may collect and if the fee is reasonable. What's reasonable? Hard to answer that question. It has a lot to do with your experience, training and your marketability. A manager takes you step by step, guiding you and your career along. He should be your partner.

A manager may decide to represent you when all that he can see is promise and it may be a long time before you will be able to secure an agent. The manager is putting faith in you that you can and will work, long before it will actually happen. I don't have a problem with that kind of a manager charging a fee in the beginning. That fee should be dropped, however, as soon as you start working. Then it should go to straight commission.

Do You Want To Be An Actor?

Actor
Cynthia Khoury

Should an aspiring actor do background work?

Yes! All work is a learning process, contributing to your career. With background work, if one makes a mistake, it won't harm your career – you'll just learn from it. Use background work to learn about, lighting, camera blocking, set etiquette and who does what and where. Watch the lead actors and learn, learn, learn.

Do You Want To Be An Actor?

Manager
Christine Low
Low Artists Management

Do managers charge the same commission as agents and should an actor pay his manager a fee?

No and yes. What do I mean by that? Managers are not under the same union regulations that agents are. So a manager may charge whatever commission the he or she negotiates with his/her client. I find that most managers charge a commission rate of about 10 – 20%.

In regards to paying a fee for representation, that would depend on the amount of experience and what name value you have that the manager can use as a marketing tool for you. If you are just coming into the business, with little or no credits, it would seem to me that it is asking a lot of the manager to take you on as a client at his/her expense, on the chance that you may make him/her and yourself a buck or two. If the fee that the manager is asking is within reason (you need to determine that), then go for it.

Do You Want To Be An Actor?

Actress
Kristine Benedict

What should an actor do if he doesn't have many credits but would like agent representation?

Do student films, as many as you can. They are a great place to learn your craft and when you have a couple of good scenes, you can put a demo tape together and you will have some credits to list on your resume. If you can, visit an agent in person – maybe you'll have an opportunity to speak with them and that could spark more interest than just a simple picture and resume.

Author's Note:

If you do plan on "dropping in" to an agency, make sure that you do it after the agents have finished with the morning submissions and before they start to make the afternoon calls. The idea of dropping in on an agent to drop off a picture and resume is not a bad idea, if you plan well in advance and if you keep in mind that the person sitting at the front desk will most likely not let you through to the agent. You could try asking the person at the front desk if you could have a moment to thank the agent for looking at your picture and resume. Most will ask the agent to step out and meet with you, if they can. If the agent is unable to, say thank you and leave the picture and resume with the receptionist with a thank you to him or her. And remember the person at the front desk may not be a receptionist at all. He or she may be the agent you're trying to reach!

Do You Want To Be An Actor?

Actor
Helene McCardle

Marketing yourself as an actor is very important. Are there specific steps that you take to get noticed and keep yourself in front of the talent buyers?

I think learning is the key. Take lots of classes, keep busy and as a result you (the actor) will be in front of talent buyers. Another step is to do free theater, it keeps the creative juices flowing and helps keep your name out there.

Do You Want To Be An Actor?

Agent
Tena Houser
Lenz Agency

When should an actor start his search for an agent?

If they want to be taken seriously by the agents at the agency, an actor should only submit after studying with a good reputable acting teacher and getting the best headshots that they can.

Do You Want To Be An Actor?

Agent
Tena Houser
Lenz Agency

Any suggestions for an actor just starting out?

Gerald Gordon and I teach a class on the Business of Show Business and give talks to many groups of people who are considering an acting career.

We suggest that people just entering this business research show business just as you would any other business or job search.

Pick up Tom Logan's book, *How to Work in the Million Dollar Minute* and Squire Fridell's book, *Prepare Yourself with Knowledge*. If someone in the business tells you something, check it out with others in the business before you act on it. Make sure it makes sense. If it's too good to be true maybe it is too good. Use your common sense.

Going into Show Business is just like going into any other technical field. To be good at it you must study. Would you trust a dentist that has never been trained to pull a tooth? I DON'T THINK SO! In the same vein, would you expect a director to take a chance on an untrained actor? Remember, a film production is very expensive and an untrained person can cost the production a lot of money. When your opportunity comes along you must be prepared with the tools of your trade: training, photographs, resumes and a demo tape. Use the proper types of photographs, have your resume typeset in proper theatrical resume format (get the author's book, *Actors' Resumes: The Definitive Guidebook*) and get a good demo tape made. Remember your photograph and resume are your business card, but most important is training. Call around to check out acting teachers. Ask them for a resume and a list of some of the students that they have had in their classes. Ask yourself, what makes this acting teacher qualified to instruct actors. Use the internet to gain all the information that you can. Call the SAG franchised agents to see who they might suggest to you for photographs and acting coaches. Train in your

Do You Want To Be An Actor?

city with everyone who has a good reputation. We like to suggest that actors do not stay with the same acting coaches for a long time as you risk becoming a clone of that one teacher's technique.

After you have prepared yourself in your local market and you feel that you are now ready to move up to a larger market, keep the following in mind:

1. Do not pick the first photographer or acting coach that you interview with.

2. Attend group settings with other actors or inexpensive seminars. Check out the colleges in the area for classes (often taught by major industry professionals). Go to the SAG seminars and ask questions.

3. Visit the trade bookstores, Samuel French, Drama Books, Performing Arts Books and others. Buy as many books on acting as you can. Read everything! You will gain a tremendous amount of information.

4. Read the trades: Back Stage, Back Stage West, The Hollywood Reporter, Variety, Drama –Logue and others.

5. Network. Be open to learn.

6. Have fun. Be cautious. Use your common sense. Prepare and study!

Do You Want To Be An Actor?

Manager
Jami and Rusty Feuer
Fire Comm Management

Do you have any suggestions for an actor preparing to move to New York or Los Angeles in search of an acting career?

Be prepared!

1. Take a very honest and hard look at yourself. What market do you fall into? Are you, Character, Leading, Juvenile, etc.? In my opinion, the market on character actors is getting very tough. Although movie budgets are going up, most of the money is going to the name stars, which means character actors are making less money overall. This makes it harder for an agent to get you (the character actor) work and to make a profit. That makes it harder for you to get an agent. You will find that you may have a much better chance of getting an agent if you are young, talented and good looking. Be honest. How hard are you willing to work?

2. If you are prepared to work hard, try to get your SAG card before coming to LA. This will help you get an agent.

3. Try to get some good tape on yourself. Agents will ask for it.

4. Get excellent photographs of yourself; make sure they represent you and your personality. Leave the fancy "Do-Da" photos for Mom's fireplace mantle.

5. Remember, if it sounds too good to be true... it probably is! Be smart. Don't leave your money with the quick fix artists. Ask questions and get your answers from reputable sources.

Good Luck!

Do You Want To Be An Actor?

Manager
Jami and Rusty Feuer
Fire Comm Management

What types of acting classes should a new actor take?

I recommend a good cold reading and/or audition course with a reputable teacher. Since it is highly unlikely that you will be cast in a big role when you are first starting out, this will prepare you for the under-five roles that you may be offered. If you can afford a cold reading class and a scene study class . . . all the better.

When choosing a scene study class, look for a teacher that inspires you to create and express your individuality and honesty. Some teachers literally take the life out of an actor's work, leaving the actor stiff, stilted and unbelievable. Do not become an "actornoid!"

Do You Want To Be An Actor?

Acting Coach
Jared Barclay

Do you believe that an actor should "dress" the part for an audition?

For commercial auditions – yes. They are all about instant consumer identification, so that products can be sold without viewer confusion.

For theatrical auditions – on all levels from meeting the casting director to the director and producers – help them see you in the role. Dress appropriately for the role but don't be literal, i.e. you shouldn't wear a badge if you're being considered for the role of a policeman. Find the essence of your character and at the audition offer all the components of your character. Don't be literal but don't also assume that people in this business are possessed with imagination.

Do You Want To Be An Actor?

Acting Coach
Jared Barclay

Are there any exercises, physical or mental, that you go through, or can suggest an actor do, before a performance or audition, to channel nervousness into positive energy?

Get off yourself. You are not the event; you are part of the event. "They" are more nervous then you are. "They" have more at stake than you do. Get rid of the critic, judge or director in your head. Dismiss the nervousness out of your consciousness during your auditions. Tell it to leave town. Visualize the nervousness disappearing. When it's gone, do your acting preparation, if the nervousness tries to come back, fire it from your audition.

Breathe. Actors forget to breathe. If you take your concentration off your nerves and place it on your slow peaceful breathing – inhalation and exhalation – you will back off yourself and will instead concentrate on your work and fulfill the intentions of the work you intend to do.

Do You Want To Be An Actor?

Coach
Annie Kidwell
Florida Actors Handbook

Do you believe that an actor should "dress" the part for an audition?

The goal of the actor going into the audition is to convince casting that he is the one right for the role. The actor must find original, interesting ways to make himself stand out from all the other actors auditioning. One of the ways to do that is to "dress the part". I believe it is more important to portray the essence of the role, rather than go to a lot of expense to costume yourself for an audition. There are others, I'm sure, that would argue that the costume is very effective.

Run though a brief check list first. How much time do you have to prepare? Can you wardrobe yourself, within reason, and still leave yourself plenty of time to prepare for the role? It doesn't make much sense to run around scaring up a costume and not spending the time learning your lines or preparing all the possible choices for your audition. Can you wear something that suggests the character versus a full costume? We really don't have the concept of the art director, so we can't fully anticipate what he and the director might want.

Think about what props you may be able to use that will add to the audition *without endangering anyone*. These are just a few of the things to consider.

The other perspective to consider is the casting director. If you know that a particular casting director prefers seeing talent dressed in costume, well, is there any doubt on what you should do? Each talent buyer has a personal preference – try to familiarize yourself with each of them.

Do You Want To Be An Actor?

Coach
Annie Kidwell
Florida Actors Handbook

How can an actor find a good acting coach or acting class?

As the publisher of a handbook for actors/models, I get asked this all the time. Training boils down to being a very personal issue, besides a monetary one. No one wants to throw money away, but the issue of what you're paying for a class should not be the deciding factor. Some of the best training may be relatively cheap.

Questions that the actor needs to ask are:

Where am I in this business (beginner, have worked some, have worked a lot, where is my market experience – national, local, regional, none)?

What kind of work do I do? Or want to do (commercials, film, television, live performances, industrials)?

What do I feel are my strengths regarding auditioning?

What about callbacks, cold readings, and performing?

What are my weaknesses? This requires some honest evaluation and maybe a consultation with people that work with you and know you well, someone whose opinion you trust.

What kind of training will benefit me now and what can I put on my calendar for the future that will benefit me in the long run?

After assessing themselves, the talent then needs to select 4-6 training venues in their area and check the classes out, ask to audit one.

Do you like the location? The studio? What level are the other

Do You Want To Be An Actor?

actors at? Along with this you should interview with the acting teacher or coach. Mind you I said the coach, not the sales rep., manager, or whatever they may be called.

Some of the best ways of finding out who is teaching, the what, where and how, is by networking with fellow actors. Ask them what classes they are currently taking or what classes have they taken? What did they get out of it? How did they feel about the coach? The other actors? Keeping in mind it's a subjective opinion. Since this is a networking and personality business, you will get a good cross-section of opinions from fellow actors.

Sometimes the raw beginner, who doesn't have many contacts to network with, just has to jump in and make a commitment to train. Pick a class that provides basic orientation and training to the business, perhaps starting with an auditioning workshop. While involved, keep your eyes and ears open for information of any kind about the business and go from there.

A six week class is not a lifetime commitment. Let me put it another way, you're not going to ruin your life or career by one choice. A word of caution, however, be very careful about any program (acting school) that wants you all to themselves, or claims to be "the only method", or intimidates you in any way (apart from the exploration process of discovering your inner feelings), or generally wants to control and direct your whole career.

Another good way to gain knowledge is to become part of a theater group. This not only provides excellent training, it's a great way to network.

We all have different "instruments" and varied needs to develop and fine-tune. There is not one path for all individuals. Use a lot of common sense in your business decisions and keep in mind that this is "the Business of Show Business". The one product you are marketing is YOURSELF.

Do You Want To Be An Actor?

Agent
Bert Charles
The Charles Talent Agency

What is the difference between "Commercial" representation and "Theatrical" representation?

Basically, "commercial" representation is where an agent is representing actors for television commercials and/or commercial print work. Many agencies will specialize in this field and only represent people for commercials, working primarily with commercial casting directors.

The agent will probably get the "Commercial Express", a service provided in Los Angeles by the Breakdown Services Ltd. This service provides the agent with all the necessary information regarding upcoming commercials. For example, "John Smith of Smith and Associates is casting a national Pepsi commercial, seeking males 25 or older with dark features, leading man quality, good with copy, and no commercial conflicts."

The agent then submits the appropriate talent (pictures and resumes), hopefully obtaining audition appointments

Theatrical representation is very similar. The difference is that the agent will represent and submit people for television shows, industrial films, soap operas, films, plays etc... The Breakdown Services also have "breakdowns" for theatrical agents and it is similar, but there is much more involved.

Breakdown Services, Ltd. Provides agents registered with the actors unions (SAG, AFTRA, or WGA, DGA) with synopses of scripts to be cast. It includes character descriptions and storylines for Feature Films, Episodic Television Shows, Movies for Television (MOW's), Mini-Series, Pilots, Cable Television Projects, and Plays.

Do You Want To Be An Actor?

Actor
Christopher Armbrister

What type of classes do you suggest a new actor take?

If you've never had an acting class, then I think you need to explore the various approaches to acting. Investigate all the options that are out there . . . ask around about different classes, then go and audit several and find one in which you feel comfortable.

Acting is a very personal expression and you must eventually discover and create your own style or "method" . . . one that is as individual and unique as you are. In the early stages of your development find an approach that makes sense to you and learn as much as possible about it and every other technique you come in contact with. Then mutate it into your own style . . . pulling bits and pieces from all of the techniques you've learned. It's best to have a good solid knowledge of the acting basics first, and then learn how to apply them in the different media.

Once you've gotten a good stranglehold on acting, then check into a camera technique class and make the necessary adaptations to your style for on-camera acting.

Finally, NEVER STOP!

You should always be in a class or workshop of some sort (be it film technique, an acting approach, method, scene study, or whatever), not only will you meet other actors and are able to network, but it keeps your instrument and skills sharp and honed.

The only reason to not be in a class is that your career (acting) keeps you so busy you literally don't have the time because you are always on the set, stage, or rehearsing.

Do You Want To Be An Actor?

Actor
Christopher Armbrister

Are there any exercises, physical or mental that you go through before a performance or audition to channel your energy or nervousness into positive energy?

I have created for myself a system, or rather a checklist, of questions and positive reinforcement statements to help me relax, hone in on my character, and keep focused in the moment. I originally developed it for auditions, but by expanding the principles I realized it also helps in sharpening all my performance situations.

EVR: C-110

Energy:
Is my energy level 100%?
Get it even higher and more specifically focused!

Voice:
Listen to the voice of the character (As he speaks to me & through me–make them one and the same).
What are his ATTITUDES & OPINIONS?
Special character attributes?
Find the humor (It's always there)!

Risk:
Focus on 2-3 *strong* choices (No more, no less. Minor subtleties will follow).
Maximum justified push (Push the envelope of your choices)!
Respond fully to *every impulse!*
Do these choices bring out the strengths of the character, while maintaining honesty and vulnerability?

Do You Want To Be An Actor?

Commitment:

Am I pushing the envelope of my choices to the maximum in every way possible?
What else can I do to get 110% out of each choice and moment?
Make 'em secure & knock 'em dead!

Do You Want To Be An Actor?

Tony Award Nominated Actor
Jekyll & Hyde
Robert Cuccioli

How should an actor prepare for an interview with a director, agent, manager or casting director?

Learn everything there is to know about that individual!

Directors:

What have they directed before? Did you see any of their work? What was your opinion about it?

Hopefully, you like their work and you have good things to say. If so, be specific. As much as you would like these people to be informed about you and your work, to be able to talk intelligently and respectfully about you, they would respect you more if you did the same for them. Find ways where their style of directing and your style of acting parallel (This is why we would work so well together).

Agents, Managers:

As difficult as it is to remember, THEY WORK FOR YOU. Interview *them*. If you don't know their history, ask: What agency or management firm were they with before? Why did they leave? How long have they been in the business? What did they do before? Were they actors themselves at one time? What is their philosophy on acting? What is their philosophy on how to promote you? How are they going to work for you?

Before you ask any of these questions you need to do some homework on yourself. Don't let someone else define you. Be realistic about yourself: know what you do, what you want to do, your goals – where do you want to be and what do you want to be doing in 1 year, 5 years, 10 years – who are you and what is it about you that is so unique? Be excited about yourself and your own prospects and they will be too.

Do You Want To Be An Actor?

Casting Directors:

Much the same as the above. Keep records of what they have cast in the past and what projects they may be doing in the future. Keep records of when you auditioned for them in and know what to expect when you go in again

Final Note:

Don't be afraid to talk about yourself. God forbid, but you do have interests other than acting. Don't you??? Well, so do these people. I wouldn't bring an obscure subject up out of the blue, but if there is an opening, go for it. You'd be surprised how warm the conversation can get when they discover you may share other interests. Be yourself and try to treat it as an adventure. Meeting new and interesting people *can* be fun. Allow it to be. True, these people may be able to further your career, but you know, your life is *not* hanging in the balance.

Do You Want To Be An Actor?

Tony Award Nominated Actor
Jekyll & Hyde
Robert Cuccioli

What suggestions do you have to actors who become very nervous at auditions?

OK, you've done your homework. You know the scene or the monologue. You've decided on what to wear and you're dressed to kill. When you get into the room, as far as you're concerned, it becomes about the work. Take your attention off yourself and put it on the person you're reading with or on the person you're saying your speech to. You made choices when you left the house. Stick to 'em. Unless, of course there are adjustments that you're asked to do on the spot. If so, just keep your cool, put the adjustments in the program and then put the attention *back* in the scene and the person you're reading with. If you feel you should have worn something else or shaved your head. Too late. If you keep your focus on the work and show what a good actor you are, even if you don't get the job, there will be a next time.

Do You Want To Be An Actor?

Acting Coach/Consultant
Tony Varro
President Act – Net / The Actors Networking Group

What should an aspiring actor do to prepare for a move to New York or Los Angeles?

A new actor should get as much experience where they currently live as possible – before trying to move to the major markets. Every metropolitan area has opportunities to work in local commercials, industrials and films. There are also excellent classes being offered in many areas of the country. Here on the west coast of Florida, my company, *The Actors Network Group* offers very good classes on how to get started in the business and what to do on an audition.

Do You Want To Be An Actor?

Acting Coach/Consultant
Tony Varro
President Act – Net / The Actors Networking Group

What should an aspiring actor do to prepare for a move to New York or Los Angeles?

After one has good training and experience, it is a good idea to try to get a SAG card in their local market before moving to NYC or LA.

Do You Want To Be An Actor?

Acting Coach/Consultant
Tony Varro
President Act – Net / The Actors Networking Group

What types of classes should an actor who is just coming into the business take?

If the actor is interested in doing work in commercials, television, or films, then the actor should be careful to take on-camera classes rather than theater classes, simply because the techniques are very different. Generally things that work for theater are not appropriate for on-camera work.

In addition, I tell actors that getting the job is the hard part. Therefore, I always suggest that actors start with classes that emphasize audition technique.

Authors Note:

The difference between stage technique and the acting style required for on-camera work is generally one of "size".

On stage one generally acts to a large house. That means that the people in the last row of the balcony must be able to see the same gestures and expressions as the people in front row orchestra. Sometimes that calls for "big" acting.

For film and television, the camera is right in your face and it catches every movement, every nuance, so the actor must be conscience of his gestures and use of his voice. He must "take things down" and act with the same energy but make it "smaller".

Do You Want To Be An Actor?

Photographer
Ron Sorensen
Visual Image Design

What do you look for when shooting an actor's headshot?

An identifiable character. You want to work? Make it easy for the talent buyers to categorize you. Yes, it may be type-casting yourself, but you will work. After you've established yourself, you can show more of a range. When being photographed always think strong image type. You will set yourself apart from the competition.

Do You Want To Be An Actor?

Director
Kevin Robert McDermott
Center Stage LA
Theatrical Workshops for the Young Professional

What should an aspiring actor do to prepare for a move to NYC or LA to seek out an acting career?

Take classes and connect to people who have a reputation. Don't pay people for advice. You can find terrific advice when you talk to people known in the business.

Do You Want To Be An Actor?

Director
Kevin Robert McDermott
Center Stage LA
Theatrical Workshops for the Young Professional

How can an actor or parent of a child actor find a good acting coach or acting classes?

For children and teens you should contact a children's agent and ask them for a name or two of reputable coaches who specialize in children.

Do not go to the type of places that blitz the media with ads. Go to an acting school that is so well respected that it does not need to bring in hundreds of people at astronomical prices.

Do You Want To Be An Actor?

Actor
Pat Lach

How should an actor prepare for an interview with a director, agent, manager or casting director?

The same as for any job interview – whether he or she is the interviewer or the interviewee.

1. Have an extra copy of your resume firmly attached to your headshot.

2. Arrive on time and allow for traffic jams, getting lost and a final "fluff up" before going in.

3. Know what you're there for:
   The role – about the role.

   Is it film, television or stage?

   The agency – if an agent interview. The size of the agency, client list, number of clients, types of actors the agency handles, areas of representation. Have questions that you would like answered.

   Know something about the person you are about to interview with.

   Dress appropriately

   I've often been told that with talent buyers it can come down to the answer to this one simple question, "Will I like working with this person?" If you were the talent buyer – how would you answer?

Do You Want To Be An Actor?

Actor
Pat Lach

Do you prefer to work with an agent, a manager or both?

I like to have an agent before finding a manager. I don't want to be put into a box regarding my talent and I don't want to be connected with a manager who fits the Hollywood stereotype. I am not opposed to having both.

Do You Want To Be An Actor?

Actor
Lance Taubold

Do you prefer working with an agent, a manager or both?

I think having both is the ideal situation for me. I have had several different agents but only one manager, Greg Barrett of Greg Barrett and Associates. He works very closely with me in all aspects of my career. And I have even gone a considerable length of time without an agent, keeping only my manager. It's worked great.

Do You Want To Be An Actor?

Photographer
Michael Papo
Michael Papo Photography

How should an actor go about choosing a photographer?

See three different photographers. All of their work will probably be good. Prices can vary from low to very high. If you like the photographer and their work – shoot with him or her. Don't fuss with the prices – it's a waste of time and energy. If you feel it's right – go for it. It's like picking a best friend for two to three hours. If you can't find a "best friend" after looking at three different photographers, check out three more.

Do You Want To Be An Actor?

Photographer
Michael Papo
Michael Papo Photography

What do you look for when shooting an actor's headshot?

I look to their eyes first. Do I get the feeling they're saying something? Is it clear? I look for the essential essence or "beingness." I want to see where their heart really is – not the image but the truth.

These qualities can be communicated in a leather jacket, a sundress, a suit or a vest and a T-shirt. The essence of the actor's personality plus the wardrobe makes a fantastic headshot.

99% of my clients have gotten paid hundreds and even thousands of dollars and my photos of them got them in the door. It should be a team effort, photographer and client – that is a win-win situation.

Do You Want To Be An Actor?

Photographer
Ed Freeman
Ed Freeman Photography

What do you look for when shooting an actor's headshot?

When an actor tries to "look" a certain way in front of the camera – dramatic, sexy, sincere, etc. – what you end up with, almost invariably, is a picture of someone "trying." The only person who would try to look sexy, sincere or dramatic is someone who isn't. So it backfires.

What I tell my subjects to do is, sit there, look at the camera and do nothing. Being in front of a still camera is not the same as being in front of a movie camera. All the subtlety and nuance has to show up in one frame. The best way to have it show up, to let it out, is to do nothing.

Of course I pay attention to camera angles and lighting to minimize long noses, double chins and uneven eyes. But mostly what I look for is that moment when all the artificialness drops away and the spirit comes shining through. For me that is the most compelling portrait.

Do You Want To Be An Actor?

Photographer
Ed Freeman
Ed Freeman Photography

How should an actor go about choosing a photographer?

1. Meet with at least 3 or 4 photographers.

2. Choose a photographer who specializes in theatrical headshots, not portraits, weddings, etc.

3. Choose a photographer you feel comfortable and relaxed with.

4. You get what you pay for – cheap photographers usually produce cheap work.

5. Be very clear about the extent and nature of your guarantee.

6. The only cities in the US where there is an abundance of qualified theatrical headshot photographers are New York and LA, [Chicago], if at all possible, wait until you can get to one of these cities before having your headshot done.

Do You Want To Be An Actor?

Photographer
Nancy Spatola
Spatola Designer Images

What do you look for when shooting an actor's headshot?

We always invite the actor in to our studio for a no cost, no obligation consultation. It is important to us to weed out the actor "wannabes." If we feel an actor's bottom line is price, we recommend that they check out other photographers. We feel quality is very important. We also look to see if they are really serious about acting, not just, "Oh my friends tell me I look good so I thought I should get into the biz." Are they willing to make a commitment work hard, go to auditions, interview agents and managers, etc.? If yes, then they may be a good client for us. If no, then we send them on their way.

Do You Want To Be An Actor?

Photographer
Nancy Spatola
Spatola Designer Images

How should an actor go about choosing a photographer?

An actor should meet the photographer beforehand to see if their personalities click. Ask yourself if this is the person you want to spend time with, while having your pictures taken?

The actor should not choose a photographer based simply on price. Price alone is not an indication of quality. Check out the work of the photographer. Make sure it's good. Ask questions. Will the photographer listen to my input? Will they shoot outside as well as studio shoots? What's the style the photographer uses?

The actor needs to know what he or she is looking for in a picture. What kind of work are you going after, film, sit-com, dramatic stage.

An actor's headshot and resume is often their first contact with the talent buyer and the picture and resume needs to represent you. This is your calling card. Do not skimp on quality. The cheapest photographer well may be the least qualified! Do they offer a guarantee that you will like the finished product . . . not just your agent, but YOU? A photographer cannot guarantee a third party will approve of the photos, especially if the agent refuses to give any input.

Do You Want To Be An Actor?

Manager
Beacon Artists Group
Lisa Ferguson

Tell us about a major no-no that actors do at an interview with you?

They come in and apologize. Whether it's an interview with an agent or manager or an audition for a casting director or producer – don't come in with an apology, i.e. *I only had a chance to look over the sides once,* or *I didn't get the call from my agent until this morning, so I'm not really ready to audition.* We – the talent buyers – don't want to know about your problems. Just do the work and make it the best you can do. We all have off days, but if you do the best you can, the casting director, agent or manager is going to see that there is talent there and they will work with you.

Do You Want To Be An Actor?

Los Angeles Casting Director

What should an actor do to get in the door to a casting director if he or she doesn't have many credits?

I suggest that every actor start out by sending in a picture and resume. You never know what I may be casting at any particular time and your picture and resume may come in to me at the perfect moment.

Send postcards, the kind with your picture on it, to remind me of a television show that you may be on or a film or play you may be in.

If you have someone in the industry that has some clout, have them call to recommend you.

Do You Want To Be An Actor?

Casting Director
Anonymous

Should an actor "dress the part" for an audition?

Hint at the character. For film and television don't come in dressed as the character. We want to hire an actor not a character. For commercials it is more acceptable to come to the audition in character.

Do You Want To Be An Actor?

Casting Director
Anonymous

What should an actor expect at a call back?

For the initial audition we call in, if time permits, about twenty actors for each role. After the first audition we call back from the first group of actors three to five actors for each part. At the call back we try to work with the actors to bring them closer to what the producers want. I give them adjustments and we go over the sides. From this group we call in two or three actors to go to producers.

Author's Note:

This is the ideal situation taking into account that the casting director has all the time in the world. More likely, the actors that the casting director likes from the first audition will be called back directly to the producers. This is known in the business as "going to producers." And try as they may, at most auditions the casting director has very little time to give more than one adjustment to the actor. The moral of the story – go to an audition knowing your stuff!

Do You Want To Be An Actor?

Chicago Casting Director

Once an actor has made contact with a casting director, how do you suggest they keep in touch?

Do not call! Let me say that again. DO NOT CALL!

Send us notes – brief notes – not pages of what you have been up to.

Send picture postcards.

Send a new headshot – if it's different from the one that we currently have.

Do You Want To Be An Actor?

Los Angeles Casting Director

What do you look for in an actor's picture and resume?

I want see something in the eyes. Sell me on the essence of you, not on what you think is selling now.

Don't get headshots that make you look like Jeff Bridges when you look more like Chris Farley. Be yourself. If you have an edge, get it in the picture. If you're beautiful, let me see it. If you're character, great! I hate it when an actor comes into an audition and looks nothing like his or her picture. It wastes my time and the actors.

Do You Want To Be An Actor?

Casting Director
Anonymous

Does an actor have to be in New York or Los Angeles to make it big?

Let's be honest. There is plenty of work in quite a few cities throughout the country, Miami, Orlando, and Chicago, just to name the major sites. But if you want to be a working actor or if you have stars in your eyes – you have to be in New York or Los Angeles.

Do You Want To Be An Actor?

Florida Casting Director

What is a "pre-read?"

Lots of actors, lots of time, that's a pre-read.

When a casting director is beginning to cast a new project and he has a lot of time, if he wants to meet with actors that he has not had the opportunity to meet with or actors he hasn't seen in a long time, he calls them in for a pre-read. It's not an actual audition for a specific part but rather a chance to read for the casting director in consideration for an audition for a specific role in the upcoming project.

Do You Want To Be An Actor?

New York City Casting Director

What should an actor expect at a "general" with you?

A general is different from a pre-read or an audition, in that, although you may be asked to read, you are in the casting directors office because he or she wants to meet you.

Most of the time I just have a nice talk with the actor. I get to know him or her a little. If they are interesting to me or I think that they fit what I'm looking for when casting then I'll have them back to audition.

Do You Want To Be An Actor?

New York City Casting Director

What is a "cold reading?"

The initial audition that a casting director calls an actor in for is in effect, a cold reading. A true cold reading is when sides are given to the actor and the actor is not given much time to study the scene before he is asked to read it. Some acting coaches specialize on teaching their actor students to pick up sides that they have not had the chance to look at and simply read them. Try to do it. It's not as easy as you think.

Do You Want To Be An Actor?

Producer / Director
Myrl Schreibman

Should an actor use color photos?

No! Why waste the money? With the advent of digital it is much more acceptable and affordable. But for print, I'd say no.

Do You Want To Be An Actor?

Producer / Director
John Lant

What type of 8 by 10's do you prefer from actors?

I like 3/4 shots. They show me more of the actor and give me a better sense of what he or she really looks likes. I like simple shots without animals or props, maybe a chair or stool but no more than that. Black and white pictures are just fine. I don't care if the picture is a lithograph or on photographic paper, but I don't like the glossy pictures that show all of the finger prints from everyone who has ever touched the picture.

Do You Want To Be An Actor?

Los Angeles Television Director

Once cast, may an actor make changes in the script or must he/she say the words exactly as written?

Exactly as written – no. But you may not change the writing unless the writer says ok to the changes. Actors may add those little "ahhs" and "ohhs" and "listens" etc., without asking, it is okay to make it your own, but do so with permission.

For example, if a line reads, "I was walking out the door when the idea *struck* me." And you feel more comfortable saying, "I was walking out the door when the idea *hit* me," I doubt anyone would have a problem with that. But, if the same line read, "I was walking out the door when the idea *struck* me." And you come out with, "I was walking out the door when, *all of sudden out of nowhere this really great thought just popped into my head*." Then we would have a problem.

Do You Want To Be An Actor?

Film Director / Producer
Norbert Misel
American Film

What might an actor expect at an interview with you?

 I rarely interview actors, unless I'm thinking of someone for a specific part. Then it's usually over lunch or dinner and it's quite casual. We just talk. Remember that when I cast an actor in a film of mine I'm casting someone who is – in essence – the character. So when I meet with an actor it is generally to confirm my feelings that he or she is right for my project.

Do You Want To Be An Actor?

Film Director / Producer
Norbert Misel
American Film

If an actor is coming in to read for you, what should he bring in terms of material?

Nothing, unless I've sent him the script already. Otherwise, after we talk, I'll give him some sides and will work them.

Monologues and prepared scenes mean almost nothing to me. I can get even the worst actor to give a good reading if I work with him on the scene long enough. When an actor comes to me with a prepared scene or monologue, I always ask them how long they've been working on it and with whom. I want to see what the actor can do with the material on an immediate basis.

Do You Want To Be An Actor?

Television and Stage Director/Producer
Heather Graham

What might you suggest that a new actor do to market himself to the talent buyers?

Getting cast in something would be by the best way for any actor to be seen. Now I know that's easier said than done. Pictures and resumes and a demo tape are also excellent. Short of that, take acting classes or scene study classes or cold reading classes that are taught by directors, agents or casting directors. Sure it's sort of like paying to meet these people, but if you want to get to know them, it's a sure bet.

Do You Want To Be An Actor?

Theatrical Director
Anonymous

Does an actor need to be in LA or New York City to make it big?

Yes. You can get work as an actor almost anyplace. But to make it big, and I assume that means making a living as an actor, you need to be in LA or New York or even Chicago to a lesser degree.

Do You Want To Be An Actor?

Producer / Director
Myrl Schreibman

What does a producer do?

What don't we do? That might be the better question. It's tough to answer because producers in different venues do different things. Film, television and stage producers, in effect, are the people who put the team together and then oversee everything that takes place within the production. I may hire and fire the cast, crew and writers. I may even be called on to write myself. Some of us direct. Think about it this way, "What needs to be done?" We either do it ourselves or find the people who will do it. We're the generals and everyone else is a soldier.

Do You Want To Be An Actor?

Television Producer
Heather Graham

Where can a parent or guardian find out about child labor laws and the entertainment industry if they are going to pursue a career for their child?

First thing any parent should do is contact their state offices to find out what requirements or restrictions there are for children working in their particular state. Then check out local book stores for books on the subject. There are plenty of good books out there on acting and what you need to know. Call the film office of your city or state. They are often an excellent source of information and the people who staff these offices are very friendly and helpful. Also, talk to other parents who might have kids in the business. And get your children to acting classes. You'll be able to network there.

Do You Want To Be An Actor?

Producer
Kimberly Price

Where do you draw the line at actors making contact with you?

I don't mind having actors or writers or directors or choreographers or any talent in the business approaching me when I'm at a social gathering or at a business affair. But when I'm at dinner with friends or family or at the park with my dog, unless I let you know that it's okay to talk shop, let's not.

Do You Want To Be An Actor?

Producer / Director
Myrl Schreibman

Where do you draw the line on actors making contact with you?

I don't mind any one approaching me to pitch an idea, whether it be to sell yourself to me to use you as an actor in my next TV show or to pitch an idea for a show, as long as it's during business. But don't ever show up at my door with a great idea you just couldn't wait to tell me about or to personally drop off a picture because you are perfect for a role on the show I'm directing. Hard to believe – but it happens.

Do You Want To Be An Actor?

Casting Director
Anonymous

Where do you draw the line on actors making contact with you?

Use common sense. Don't just drop by the office or my home or where I park my car. Remember we're in the business of show business. Treat it and everyone like it's a business. Be professional.

Do You Want To Be An Actor?

Manager
Christine Low
Low Artists Showbiz Kidz

Where do you draw the line on actors making contact with you?

Contact me through the usual routes. Call or send me a flyer to invite me to a showcase or to let me know if you're on some TV show or in a film. But don't call me at home at midnight because you were sure you'd catch me in. I don't really mind if you approach me at a restaurant, as long as you see that I'm not deeply engaged in conversation with my guests. If you do stop by the table make it brief and be polite. Gifts from people I know are wonderful and appreciated, but a gift from an actor that I briefly met one night at a cocktail party only makes me feel guilty and embarrassed. It makes me think, "Great! Now I feel obligated to call you in." You might think then that it worked. Sure, you got called in, but you can bet that most of the time I'll never sign you. Why would I? You've made me feel guilty and embarrassed every time I think about you.

Do You Want To Be An Actor?

Manager
Lyon Roberts

Where do you draw the line on actors making contact with you?

Don't monopolize my time wherever it is that we meet. At parties or after a class that I may be teaching, are great times to chat. But not at my office, unless I've called you in and not when I'm at a meeting with someone else. I've met a lot of people at industry networking parties, which I think are great, and through friends. That's a very safe place to make contact.

Do You Want To Be An Actor?

Producer / Director
Adam Roake
AFI

What should an actor expect at an audition with you?

At a producers' session, there is usually me, the director, the writer, several other producers – in the room along with you and the casting director. It can be quite a room full. The talent comes in. He is introduced to us and then he gives his reading. Sometimes we will ask for it again with a slight change and sometimes we will really work the scene. But most often, the actor will read for us and then we move on to the next one. After the session we make our decision on which talent we would like for each role. We also choose a backup for each role in case our first choice is unavailable.

Do You Want To Be An Actor?

Producer
Athanasia "Zee" Vrinios

If an actor has blonde hair and you need a brunette, would you have any problems with him or her changing their hair color before coming in?

Yes and no.

Yes, if we have already seen the actor for a specific part and we are asking him to come back in.

No, as long as the new hair color fits the description of what the character is.

I would strongly suggest that, before any actor change anything from the way he or she looks in his 8 by 10, he contact the casting director and ask first.

Author's Note:

This is assuming that the actor has already auditioned and is now going to producers. The rule of thumb here is, in between the time that you initially auditioned and the time that you are called back. If you've changed your look in any way, let the casting director know.

Do You Want To Be An Actor?

Producer
Athanasia "Zee" Vrinios

Once cast, can an actor make any changes in the script or must he follow it exactly?

The actor does not need to follow the script word for word, although he should try to stay very close to the writer's original words. Now I'm speaking for film and television where actors will often substitute a word or two that, through the rehearsal, we (the producers and director with the writer's permission) have found might work better. With stage plays or musicals, I understand that every change needs to be approved by the writer. After all it is he or she that created the character you are now acting out. Most writers I've worked with understand the needs of an actor and are most willing to work with you.

Author's Note:

You need to know that the writer is the only person who can legally make any changes to his or her material unless he has sold or assigned his rights.

Do You Want To Be An Actor?

Producer
John Lant

What might you suggest that an actor do to prepare for a move to LA or NYC?

Save a lot of money.

Study.

Be flexible.

Do You Want To Be An Actor?

Producer
Dick Woody
Casey/Woody Entertainment

What can an actor do to market himself to talent buyers?

Other than the usual route of submitting pictures and resumes, keep in front of the talent buyers by any means possible. Do free theater, paid theater, comedy, improvisational theater. Take classes. Get innovative in a non-threatening way. What do I mean by that? Think of a great cover letter or mail your picture and resume in a unique envelope. Cut a great demo. Get noticed.

Do You Want To Be An Actor?

Producer
Gene Casey
Casey/Woody Entertainment

Should an actor dress the part for an audition?

Not when he comes in to see me.

Hint at it but please don't wear a ski mask and all black because you're reading for a terrorist. Now, all black with no ski mask – that would work.

Do You Want To Be An Actor?

Producer
Anonymous

What one big mistake do actors make when they audition for you?

Not knowing the material and then making excuses for it. Also, complaining, i.e. about the wait, the writing, the actor's agent etc. Who wants to work with someone like that?

Do You Want To Be An Actor?

Actor
Dick Martinsen

Would you hip pocket with an agent?

Sure. Why not? If he won't sign you, then at least someone is submitting you. I recently had two agents who wanted to just send out a few pictures of me during pilot season. I got to audition for several pilots and one of the agents signed me. It made things easy. And why should the agent sign you for representation before you have shown that you can audition?

Author's Note:

This isn't a bad situation for the actor. The Screen Actors Guild and the American Federation of Television and Radio Artists might have something else to say about this practice, however.

Do You Want To Be An Actor?

Actor
Shelley Parisi

How does an actor find out about auditions?

    If you are not represented by a manager or an agent, then the acting trade papers, like: *Back Stage, Back Stage West, Drama-Logue, Variety* and the *Hollywood Reporter* are the best places to look. If you don't live in New York City or Los Angeles, check your local papers as well as the library and local theaters, anywhere audition notices are placed. Another good spot is the theater department of the local colleges.

Do You Want To Be An Actor?

Casting Director
Anonymous

How do actors find out about auditions?

It depends on where you live. There are trade papers and magazines that are available nationally, such as, *Variety* and *The Hollywood Reporter* that list auditions. Also I've heard that *Entertainment Weekly* and other entertainment oriented magazines occasionally have audition notices in them. If you do respond to an audition notice in a weekly, tabloid type of magazine, I would suggest that you be very careful there. If you're not in the major markets, check with community theaters and the local television and radio stations. They sometimes know of auditions that are coming up. Also, local acting coaches and acting schools are often contacted when a production company is coming to town. Try there.

Author's Note:

One of the best places for information on what's happening in the industry in your area is your local film commission. Call information and ask for the number of the film commission office in your city or state. Ask for a copy of the production guide (most of the time it's free). Inside you will find listings for everything from Talent to Casting, Craft Services to Hotels.

Do You Want To Be An Actor?

"When you give up your dreams, you die."

Flash Dance

Do You Want To Be An Actor?

What To Do Next

Okay, you've made it this far. Hopefully many of the questions, you had about breaking into the business, have been answered on the previous pages. Undoubtedly, there are some questions that you may still have. That's fodder for the next edition of this book.

Let's briefly review what you have so far. The first thing that you should do after reading this book is do the *Where am I?* and *What am I worksheets?* Having done that – you now have an idea of your "type" and what to expect from the talent buyers when they are casting you. Your "type" is how the public views you, so use it!

Next, get out there and get some training. Go to a reputable acting coach or school and start the learning process. More important than studying with acting coaches or in an acting class is getting real experience. Start in local community theater, or a school/college production. In the beginning do all the theater that you can, even if your 18 and they want you to play 60! This is the best time for you to experiment. It's actually the only time that you're going to have the opportunity to do so, once you become a professional actor you will only be cast in roles that are your "type" so play all the different types now.

When you have some stage experience and training, put together a theatrical resume. Note, that I said a *theatrical resume*, not a business resume. An actor's resume does not look like a business resume. One sure sign of an amateur is a theatrical resume that does not fit the industry standard. Get *Actors' Resumes: The Definitive Guidebook* read it and put together a resume that will market you as an actor to the talent buyers in a completely professional manner.

Some of you out there may be questioning why you should pursue stage experience if you want to work in film and television? First, you need the experience of working in front of an audience, working with a director and on a stage. Remember before television and film there was only the stage. The theatrical terms that we use on a film or television set (a soundstage) – to tell an actor where to stand or move, come from the terms used on the legitimate stage. You will need to know these terms.

Do You Want To Be An Actor?

Perfect, you're doing great; you have experience, training and a professional theatrical resume. What's next? Get great photos. Not enough can be said about the importance of a great headshot.

Note, that I did not say a good headshot. It has to be great – really great! A headshot is everything to an actor. Every talent buyer who considers buying your talent for his or her production is going to start by looking at your headshot. If your picture doesn't catch the attention of the talent buyers and they don't turn it over – then all of the credits and training in the world won't matter, because they never saw your resume! Need I say more?

Now that you have a great headshot, a professional theatrical resume, credits and training, start to market yourself to the talent buyers. Try your local market first – check the telephone book for Theatrical Agents or Acting – submit your picture and resume to those talent buyers with a brief cover letter telling a little about yourself. Include information about the new play, commercial, or print shoot you just completed or talk a bit about your new acting coach. Don't tell the talent buyer everything in a three page letter, just a paragraph or two. Save the rest for conversation when you meet face to face.

With perseverance and a lot of luck you can make it as a working actor. It won't be easy. But, then anything that is really worth having – rarely is easy to get. I've known many actors –some have moved on to other avenues, some have made it big, you would know their names.

Sometime soon, when your name is up in lights, send me a note – I'd be happy to add you to the list of actors that *DO YOU WANT TO BE AN ACTOR?* 101 Answers to Your Questions About Breaking into the "Biz," has helped on their way.

Do You Want To Be An Actor?

List of Contributors

Armbrister, Christopher
Barclay, Jarred
Barrett, Greg
Benedict, Kristine
Boaldin, Greg
Brown, Audra J.
Butto, Carl
Campana, Frank
Casey, Gene
Charles, Bert
Cuccioli, Robert
Ferguson, Lisa
Feuer, Jami
Feuer, Rusty
Foot, Mary Rachel
Freeman, Ed
Houser, Tena
Jacobs, Judith
Johnston, Johnny
Khoury, Cynthia
Kidwell, Annie
Lach, Pat
Lant, John
Low, Christine
Martinsen, Dick
McCardle, Helene
McDermott, Kevin Robert
Misel, Norbert
Papo, Michael
Parisi, Shelley
Price, Kimberly
Renn, Grace
Roake, Adam
Roberts, Lyon
Schreibman, Myrl
Sorensen, Ron

Do You Want To Be An Actor?

Spatola, Nancy
Taubold, Lance
Urich, Tom
Varo, Tony
Vrinios, Athanasia "Zee"
Woody, Dick

Do You Want To Be An Actor?

About The Author

Richard Devin, has performed on the stage, in films and on television. He is a member of the Screen Actors Guild - SAG, American Federation of Television and Radio Artists – AFTRA, and Actors Equity Association – AEA.

A theatrical agent at two of Hollywood's top talent agencies, he represented Academy Award, Grammy Award and Emmy Award nominated and wining actors.

He has directed and produced for television and the stage.

www.ingramcontent.com/pod-product-compliance
Lightning Source LLC
Chambersburg PA
CBHW071513040426
42444CB00008B/1633